W9-AMP-315

Start TO Finish
Second Series

Food

# FROM Wheat TO Bread

STACY TAUS-BOLSTAD

 LERNER PUBLICATIONS COMPANY • Minneapolis

Lerner Publications Company
A division of Lerner Publishing Group, Inc.
241 First Avenue North
Minneapolis, MN 55401 U.S.A.

Website address: www.lernerbooks.com

**Photo Acknowledgments**
Images in this book are used with permission of:
© Manuelteles/Dreamstime.com, p. 1; © Todd Strand/Independent Picture Service, pp. 3, 13, 15, 17, 19, 21, 23; Courtesy John Deere & Company, pp. 5, 7; © Nigel Cattlin/Visuals Unlimited, Inc., p. 9; © Chris Hondros/Getty Images, p. 11.

Front cover: © iStockphoto.com/ajijchan.

Main body text set in Arta Std Book 20/26.
Typeface provided by International Typeface Corp.

Library of Congress Cataloging-in-Publication Data

Taus-Bolstad, Stacy.
    From wheat to bread / by Stacy Taus-Bolstad.
        p. cm. — (Start to finish, second series. food)
    Includes index.
    ISBN 978-0-7613-9178-4 (lib. bdg. : alk. paper)
    1. Bread—Juvenile literature. 2. Wheat—Processing—Juvenile literature. I. Title.
TX769.T3554 2013
664'.722—dc23                        2011036512

Manufactured in the United States of America
1 – DP – 7/15/12

# TABLE OF Contents

# Bread is good to eat. How is it made?

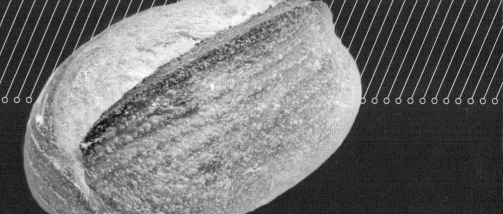

## A farmer plants wheat.

A farmer plants wheat seeds with a tractor. Sunlight and rain help the seeds grow into plants. The plants turn golden brown.

## The farmer cuts the wheat.

The farmer drives a machine called a **combine**.
The combine cuts down the plants and breaks
off the seeds.  Wheat seeds are called **kernels**.
Trucks take the kernels to a factory.

## Machines make flour.

Workers pour the kernels into machines. The machines clean and crush the kernels. The crushed kernels are pushed through a screen. Big pieces stay on top. Powder falls through. This powder is flour.

## The flour is bagged.

A machine puts the flour into bags. Trucks take some flour to grocery stores. People buy it to make bread at home. Some flour goes to factories and bakeries. Workers there make most of the bread we eat.

## A baker makes dough.

A baker puts the flour in a mixer.  Then the baker adds eggs, butter, and a yellow powder called yeast.  The mixer stirs everything together to make dough.

## A mixer stirs the dough.

The mixer keeps stirring. The dough turns into a white ball. The mixer **kneads** the dough by folding and squeezing it.

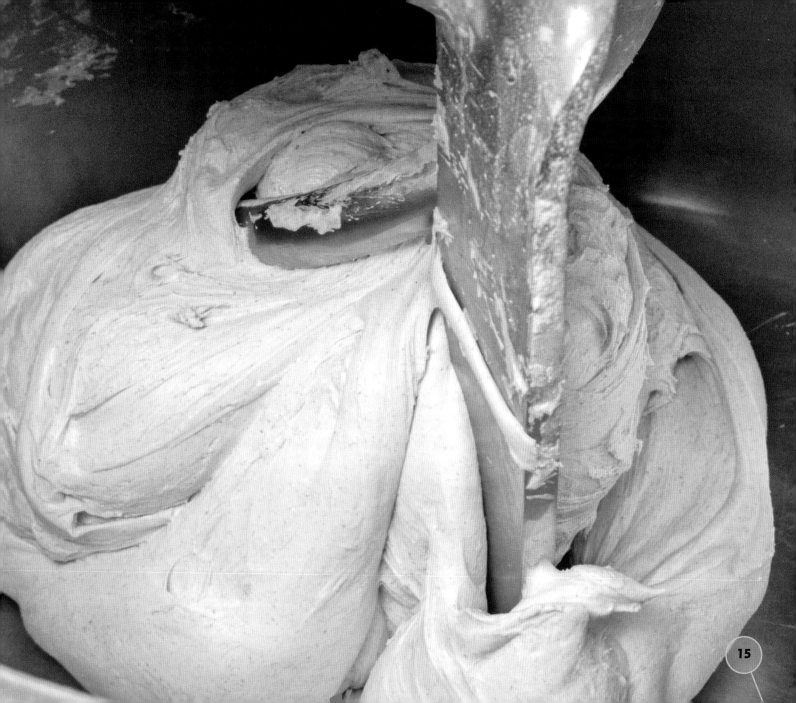

## The dough rises.

The dough sits in a bowl. The yeast makes the dough rise into a puffy ball. Without yeast, dough stays flat.

## The baker shapes loaves.

Dough is ready to be shaped after it rises. The baker shapes the dough into loaves.

## The loaves are baked.

The baker puts the loaves into a hot oven. The heat bakes them until they are light brown. When they come out of the oven, they are bread.

## Time to eat!

The farmer's tiny wheat kernels have become bread.  Try some toast with jelly. Do you like strawberry or grape?

## Glossary

**combine (KAHM-bine):** a machine used to cut wheat

**dough (DOH):** bread that has not been baked yet

**kernels (KUR-nuhlz):** wheat seeds

**kneads (NEEDZ):** folds and squeezes

**yeast (YEEST):** a yellow powder that makes dough rise

## Index